LIZA'S MONDAY

AND

OTHER POEMS

Community Enrichment Series

Appalachian Consortium Press
Boone, North Carolina

LIZA'S MONDAY

AND

OTHER POEMS

BY

BETTIE SELLERS

Library of Congress Cataloging in Publication Data
Sellers, Betty M.
    Liza's Monday and other poems

    1. Appalachian Region, Southern—Poetry.
    2. Women—Poetry. I. Title.
    PS3569.E5745L5   1986   811'.54   86-13984
    ISBN 0-913239-43-7

ACKNOWLEDGEMENTS

Acknowledgement is gratefully made to the editors and publishers of the following journals and anthologies, in the pages of which some of these poems have previously appeared: APPALACHIAN HERITAGE, BLACK JACK 11, THE CHATTAHOOCHEE REVIEW, THE GARFIELD LAKE REVIEW, GEORGIA JOURNAL, GREEN RIVER REVIEW, POEM 50, THE REACH OF SONG II, THE REACH OF SONG IV, THE REACH OF SONG, V, TEACHING ENGLISH IN THE TWO-YEAR COLLEGE.

IN LOVING MEMORY OF MY GRANDMOTHER,
COSBY SEALE PURSLEY, WHO TOLD ME
STORIES OF BRASSTOWN

Books by Bettie Sellers

WESTWARD FROM BALD MOUNTAIN 1974
APPALACHIAN CAROLS 1975
SPRING ONIONS AND CORNBREAD 1978
MORNING OF THE RED-TAILED HAWK 1981
LIZA'S MONDAY 1986

THE TIME: SOME PARTS OF THE 19TH CENTURY

THE PLACE: THE BRASSTOWN VALLEY WHICH
RUNS WEST THROUGH GEORGIA AND
NORTH CAROLINA FROM THE
HEIGHTS OF BRASSTOWN BALD

THE CHARACTERS: SOME REAL, SOME IMAGINED
FROM STORIES TOLD TO ME
BY MY GRANDMOTHER AND
OTHERS WHO HAVE LIVED IN
THE VALLEY

CONTENTS

AND ALL THE PRINCES ARE GONE

She sits beside the oak fire, Lilah, pale,
intent on nothing here where mountains circle
Brasstown tight as walls around a medieval
castle formed. She holds the book, its cover
gone, its pages tissue thin with fingering.
She peers through smoke to where the men,
their coats brocaded, satin tight around
their thighs, bow to ladies in a banquet
hall. Soft music sounds around the spitting
of the logs that Samuel dragged from Double
Knob behind his lumbering ox, a mild and
placid beast who chews his hay as though
in contemplation of the history of his kind.
She sees the ox, a Yule log chained behind,
crossing the drawbridge to a castle court,
and servants hanging holly boughs to grace
stone walls, and torches shadowing a feast.
Her cabin is not here, nor Samuel's supper
simmering on the hook above the fire. Dark
comes, and Lilah watches dancing figures spin,
a pleasant dream to warm this wilderness where
life is hard, and all the princes are gone.

CHARLIE WALKS THE NIGHT

Charlie stalks the night, dark as the painter
silent on the ridge. His bare feet touched cold
leaves with no feeling; his eyes reach only
for the phantoms of his dream. Night after night,
he travels paths never seen by Brasstown's sun.

When he was eight, his mama put the key down deep
inside a pail, sure that water's touch would wake
him gently, send him stumbling back to bed. But,
Charlie took the bucket, poured the water out,
and walked an extra mile. Then Mama tied a string

around his toe, the other end to hers, so she could
wake and keep her boy inside. She felt a little
silly when he turned sixteen, big boy like that,
and him all tied to Mama's toe. Now, Mama's gone,

and Charlie's free to walk. He never knows just
where he's been, up Cedar Ridge, or down by Big
Bald Creek where pools run dark with sleeping
trout—no sign to mark his way except the muddy
footprints on the rough pine porch, and sometimes,
scraps of Oak leaves stuck on quilts that Mama made.

SARAH'S QUILTS

She stands, barefoot, in the creek, homespun dress,
rich brown with walnut dye, tucked up almost
to knees that feel the rush, the chilling press
of Corn Creek's water even in the heat

of August. Now her sons are far away:
one running over hills his footsteps beat
on forest trails she never saw. Laurel
thickets tear his clothes, snatch hands

that picked up stones to end the quarrel
once too often, left his brother dead,
buried beneath the oak that tops the rise
just steps behind the cabin. She sees his head

rest on patchwork squares she sewed; a quilt
she made to warm his bed serves as a shroud
to line his grave. His brother's fear, his guilt
have made him run without a wrap to warm

him in the cold of mountain nights, no bright-
patched "Star of Bethlehem" to ward off harm
lurking behind great pines. She prays for brothers
as she picks up stones, piles them along the bank.

One stone, now clean of blood, joins others
she will use to lay around a space,
an outline like the rope-strung attic bed
where he can sleep, her quilt across his face.

HAWK AND JAYS

By Crooked Creek, Amanda watches as six jays
engage a sparrow hawk; their wings feinting
blue brush near his brown-barred tail
fanned wide with rage furious as his cry.
He perches wary on an oak limb, dares
further move as jays debate deep in a chinquapin.
They attack again, again in twos and threes
until the hawk, tiring of the game,
abandons territory he has claimed as his.

Amanda turns from oak leaves still quivering
after war, resumes her gathering of sticks
to feed the fire burning low on her hearth.
Above, the hawk swoops high across the valley,
dives, screaming toward her frightened chicks.
Amanda drops the wood, flaps her homespun apron:
"You wicked bird, get away from here!
Hush, hush, my biddies. Don't you be afraid!"

DON'T SEND ME OFF LIKE
SOME THREE-LEGGED DOG
In memory of Prof. Adams, who told me tales

John Lowe has gone to join his other leg,
the right one Neighbor Sam cut off with knife
and saw that February day when winds
perverse and raw as March whipped oak limbs

sideways, off from true, crushed nerve and bone
beyond repair. "Don't throw it out!" John groaned.
"Don't let me go to meet my Maker
less than whole. Don't send me off

to hop along the golded streets of Heaven
like some three-legged dog." So Sam devised
a coffin smaller than a child's; of oak
he sawed it, sealed it tight. And, while his stump

was healing, John whittled angels, tall and fair,
with flowing robes, since who knows anyhow
if angels have legs under all that heavenly garb.
The decorated coffin graced the corner

of his room for forty years while John
made do with wooden legs, another carved
when one grew splintery with plowing
rocky mountain cornfields, tending pigs.

And when the neighbors called, or strangers rode
through Brasstown, John would show his coffin,
tell about the fateful day he lost his leg.
He'd tap the lid, smooth angel's hair,

and muse how Peter's holy touch would put
his parts together once he got there,
send him off down shining streets to meet
God man-to-man, as any should. This day,

as it was told, they buried all of John,
coffin within coffin, laid him down to rest
among the oaks that shade the rising slopes
of Double Knob. The preacher, come on horseback

over Unicoi, prayed long and loud
so all could hear, and Peter surely know
what he must do when John and all his legs
comes knocking, knocking at the golden door.

PINK

Her mama called her "Pink" when she was born,
to match a tiny flower pressed in Exodus—
from Charlestown gardens, its like not found
among the blossoms wild in Brasstown soil.

She called the two boys "Flotsam" and "Jetsam,"
having heard such words ring somewhere
with all the strength of heroes: Samson, Saul—
though never could she find them in The Book

no matter if she searched to Revelation's end.
The last child Mama named "Rebecca to be sure,
make up for giving wrong names to the boys—
and those now stuck too tight to budge.

Then Mama died, not knowing just how right
she'd called her boys, hell-bent to leave the plow
and hoe for parts out West where gold grew common
as the stones they cursed in winding valley rows.

In time, their faces faded as Pink brushed
Rebecca's long red hair, the color of her own.
She washed and cooked, up on a wooden stool
that Papa made so she could reach the tubs and stove.

She stitched the gown for Rebecca's wedding day,
embroidered it with pinks and ragged robins
around the neck and sleeves. In other springs,
she knitted caps for babies never hers.

She did for Papa till his days were through
and kept the cabin neat as Mama ever could.
Alone, she withered slowly, frail and dry
as petals caught and pressed by Exodus.

AMANDA CLIMBS CEDAR RIDGE

The deepest snow in memory
clutches at my boots.
I have trudged down to the barn.
Sally lows to be milked
and the old hens cluck "cracked corn"
no matter what the day brings.

With each step, I sink, pull up,
spend my little strength.
My breath comes harder
the closer to my house I come.

Ahead of me, the snow is smooth
with no tracks but mine
splayed out like bears had walked
behind me down my daily path.

At the edge of the orchard,
a hound has padded his circle around
my tree, a juniper planted
after one Christmas. A forgotten
strand of tinsel catches sun,
reminds me of days when snow fell

only to be tossed in balls,
and stirred in pans of sweetened cream.

LEAH'S APRON

Her eastern window fogs with April frost,
obscures the cabin high across the valley
where Nathan lives alone, no smoke rising
yet, no tall man in the barnlot tending pigs.

Leah rubs the pane with her apron's calico,
blinks back as the sun rises over Kirby Cove
lighting his roof and yard, remembers springs
when Nathan came to call, a bunch of early

violets in his clumsy hand, a ring
he fashioned out of horseshoe nails, amber
honey from his hillside hives—small gifts
made large with halting words, a sober

hand raised just as he turned to leave.
But never could he say the right words
though she waited, patient, while five springs
of violets faded. She turns to face the room,

folding her apron thick to lift brown hoecake
from the fire's edge. Leah smooths her apron
with long strokes, breaks bread, and sits
down by the window to begin another day.

LOVE SONG FOR REBECCA
I. REBECCA'S PAPA

"Rebecca, bring The Book and read to me a while.
Your mama always did till you were born,
and she was gone." The tall man, petulant
beside the fire, looks back to watch her step down
from the box he built to raise a child
so she could reach the supper dishes in the pan.
She dries small hands on a bleached sack,
and, carrying the leather-covered book, comes close
to sit just by his knee. "Read Abraham again,
read how his seed will fill the land."
She follows words across thin pages with one finger
as he strokes her hair, dark like his own.
Night closes in the cabin, builds a quiet wall
around the two beside the dying fire.
"Rebecca, take my shoes off, your mama always did."
She kneels, obedient to his voice, unlaces heavy thongs
and warms his feet between her hands. "I love you,
Papa, don't be sad." He takes her in his lap.
Unbuttoning the calico around her throat, he strokes
soft flesh, rocking as the fire flickers out.

II. THE PREACHER MAN

When Papa died one spring, still calling Mama's name,
Rebecca put The Book up on the highest shelf.
No one to read to now, she thought, no one to rock me
by the fire at night. Her thirtieth year it was,
and she had never been outside the valley's walls,
had never been toward Unicoi, or west to cross through
Brasstown Gap. Her papa died still sad because his name
would have no son to carry it. She buried him
by Gumlog Creek, as near to Mama as she dared,
and drew his chair close by the fire to rock away
the chilly nights just faintly tinged by now with violets
opening by the creek. She rocked through days when sourwood
enticed the bees, and till the fingered leaves of sassafras
turned scarlet in the fall. Then through the yellow poplar
woods, a preacher man from Carolina way came riding
in his buggy, bringing sermons forged on rocky trails
in mountain nights when painters cried like women in travail,
and men could know that mortal sins were real as rocks and sky
"Rebecca, bring The Book and read to me a while," he said.
He echoed Papa's face and form, his dark beard flecked
with snow like that which fell outside the cabin walls.
He used her body sparingly, replenishing the earth as God
has said, and never knew how much she missed her Papa rocking
by the fire, unbuttoning the calico that warmed her waiting throat.

III. REBECCA'S SON

She births her son toward morning, lies there
limp, hears their whispered voices, wonders
why they do not bring him closer, let her
see. "Now, you just rest, Rebecca, sleep
a while and get your strength back, sleep."
She closes heavy eyes, still almost hearing
voices...we daren't let her know just yet...
break her heart...wonder what she done to get
so marked a boy. She sleeps, and wakening
hears morning sound, the clatter of the skillet,
the murmuring of coffee boiling in the pot.
The midwife Mary Nash, from up in Kirby Cove,
sits rocking by the fire, a swaddled
bundle quiet in her arms. Rebecca raises up:
"Mary, bring my child, and let me see his face."
Reluctant, Mary walks across the room
and lays him in the crook Rebecca makes.
Morning sun breaking through the window
touches the birthmark shiny and red. "Jehovah God,
what have I done that you should punish me?
The sins are visited upon the young, The Book
says." She lies back, bares her breast,
guides it toward the purple mouth, and with
one finger traces sin made visible,
on Enoch's cheek for him to wear for life.

IV. ENOCH PREACHES AT GUMLOG

"Jehovah God, convict these miserable sinners,
bring them to their knees." Mid-morning sun
strikes new fire from his birthmark swollen as
blue veins that pulse distended, fierce around
his eyes. "Conceived in mortal sin, we all
are filled with wickedness, dependent on
Your Mercy, damned without Your Grace. Fall
down, you sinners, put your faces on the ground."
He raises clinched fists, brings them down
to pound upon the rough-hewn pulpit he has carved
to finish off the log church crouching in the laurel
thicket close by Gumlog Creek. "Jehovah God,
forgive this miserable man who bears upon his face
the mark of Cain, the sin of Abram's seed."
He falls upon his knees, sinks clutching fingers
deep within the earthern floor, and weeps. Around him,
empty benches line up square in quiet wooded rows.

REQUIEM FOR A MATRIARCH

When Laura
Lenora
Queen Victoria
Stanfield
Brown
had fried
the last pone
of cornbread
on the black
woodstove,
her husband
and twelve children
buried her
among the laurels
head-high
by Gumlog Creek,
put no
REQUIESCAT IN PACE
on her stone.
Old Lunsford,
tired of carving,
put down his chisel
and declared:
"I do reckon
that name's enough.
Ever soul
in the county know'd
she were a good woman
and sore in need
of the rest."

EUNICE CLAIMS THE STAR OF BETHLEHEM

"It's mine! How dared you give our mother's
finest quilt to Cousin Ruth?" She fumes
around the room, her fingers touching,
clutching at the piles of many-colored quilts,
the crocheted pieces Mama made those years
when age had slowed her feet, and sat
'most too quiet by the fire. "The Star of Bethlehem
was mine. She told me so right in this very room."
Her sister, quieter still than Mama ever was,
goes on about her business, clearing cupboard
shelves, folding Mama's dresses in a pile.
"Now, don't you dare to give away another thing!
Just think how Mama'd feel, your tossing out
her very life like it was trash to burn, and her
not cold yet in her grave. Not one scrap, mind you.
Do you her me, Sister? Not one scrap!" She lifts
each folded quilt and calls its name: Step-Around-The-
Mountain, Double Wedding Ring, Flower Garden,
Sailor's Bow-Tie. "See these, I mind the very day
she finished every one and laid it on the bed
to show. And all that time, that sneaky Ruth
was casting eyes, just coveting the last stitch
Mama did. I knew it, and to think just when
my back was turned, you'd go and give away my quilt.
Well, you just leave this room, and don't come back
again! I'll move my things in here, and see you don't
throw out our Mother's life. You can sleep alone,
you hear, and don't ever speak to me again!"

MORNINGS, SHEBA COMBS HER HAIR

She watches from the open door, the man
long-legged, tall and straight, his hair aflame
like foxes make as they run through the broom
sedge patch behind her house. This neighbor
passes by each day to climb the slope
of Cedar Ridge, cut logs to build a barn
near where the trail that crosses Unicoi
turns west through Brasstown Gap.
She watches, thinking how her own man,
gone these three years, never had
that loose-limbed stride, that fire atop
his head. Older than she, he never made
her heart run wild and fly across the valley
free as red-tailed hawks rise high
on currents of cold morning air. She watches,
planning how one day she'll walk out, ask him
how his wife does, how his son. She'll wait
beside the big oak, ask him in to warm his hands
before her hearth, to notice how her dark hair falls
as smooth as water in Corn Creek caresses stones.
How she will warm cold fingers in his hair,
and face eternal burning if she must.

ENOCH'S SERMONS
I. A DAY OF CLOUDS AND THICK DARKNESS

Enoch rises, opens up The Book. Aaron drops his eyes,
turns them on his boots, not seeing worn leather toes
but Sheba's face, her dark head bent. She sits across
the church where he can see the curve of cheek he's cupped
with tender hands, the shoulders soft and warm, now masked
in Sunday calico. Beside him, Joel stirs and yawns,
his bright head drooping now against his father's side.
Enoch reads, his voice a burning pain in Aaron's mind:
abomination...thy neighbor's wife...defile...shalt not...
The words, the words...abomination...neighbor's wife.
He'd never meant to go inside, but coming down each night
from Cedar Ridge, he'd seen her standing in the open door,
smelled fragrant hickory burning on her hearth. That day,
November chilled the bright still air in Brasstown. And
he was cold. Aaron glances toward his wife, her lips
set Sunday-tight, her eyes on Enoch's purple mouth.
What if her sharp eyes looked through Sheba's calico,
her flesh? They'd see his seed, insidious, growing
wild as pigweed taints the dark soil of his garden rows.
They'd all see soon, these neighbors, friends. Aaron feels
the boy, breathing softly now in sleep. He sees his wife's
skirt move to touch his leather toes. Jehovah God, he thinks,
what will I do? But God, Oh God! I was so cold!

II. O ABSALOM, MY SON, MY SON

What did that David know? Did he once carry Absalom
inside his belly, feel his warm mouth urging milk
from full breasts swollen in hard ropes of sustenance
and pain? Watch him live a week, a month, then cease
to breathe no matter what he did? Amanda draws
her grey shawl tight across dry breasts, flabby
these many childless years. Her twisting fingers
count a row of tiny graves grown over with laurel now
by Gumlog Creek. What does that Enoch know? Him
like a eunuch with his purple face no woman would dare
touch for fear of bearing sons marked like him.
"But the king covered his face and the king cried out
with a loud voice..." Enoch reads The Book again,
tells of Joab chiding David for his grief. Amanda stirs,
glances sideways at the man whose seed was weak, that seed
so ripe and quickening until exposed to light. What
does that man know, him with his "Never you mind, Amanda.
God just didn't mean our sons to live and have to face
this wicked world." She feels her dry breasts fill again,
watches as milk trickles down her wrinkled flesh like tears.

III. THE FOUNTAIN IN THE WAY TO SHUR

Abigail sees through log walls, across
the barrier tall mountains make, to where
the sea laps on earth so warm she feels it
in her fingertips pressed against her thighs.
Fearful in this alien land of deep thickets,
painters prowling, snow, she is as Hagar
thrust into a trackless wilderness. But here,
by Gumlog Creek, no angel of the Lord has
found her, ministered to her need. How many
times has she heard Enoch promise help from
this Jehovah: a cloud by day, a pillar of fire
in deep darkness, an angel hand. And nothing
came to Abigail. If this Jehovah is so great,
how has He not seen Enoch's face, laid on
His hands to heal that purple lying mouth,
no more effective than the lying prayers
she nightly prays to One who never hears.

IV. NO BALM IN GILEAD

The church walls darken; Enoch's face fades
as though April sun had gone behind a cloud
or dropped between the peaks of Raven Cliffs.
Anna blinks her eyes, sees only mist as pain,
insistent in her side, drowns out Enoch's voice:
"Why then is not the health of the daughter
of my people recovered?" Elizabeth stirs,
touches her mother's hand: "You alright, Mama?"
Anna nods, afraid to trust speech, reveal her fear
now deeper than death: how to plant corn and peas
to feed herself, Elizabeth, when weakness comes
in waves, waves hard and round in her side
as oak roots washed to view by spring rain's fall.
How to leave Elizabeth alone, this child who cannot
learn beyond the simplest thing. The sound of Enoch's
voice returns: "Is there no balm in Gilead, is there
no physician here?" Anna closes her eyes, bows
in prayer. Elizabeth pats her mother's hand:
"Open your eyes, Mama. Mama, I can't see your eyes!"

V. NOW THE LORD HAD PREPARED
   A GREAT FISH

And Enoch reads of Jonah, disobedient to the Lord,
swallowed by the great fish. He tells of Nineveh,
and forty days to punishment. "Repent, repent of sin!"
His voice is high and thin. "Let every man be covered
with sackcloth." The congregation stirs, uneasy, feels
the weight of wrongs brought here to holy ground
disguised in piety and Sunday garb. "Come to the Lord,
repent your wickedness!" One, two, they come, then more.
They cling around the mourner's bench, curve against
the oaken rail as scales overlap on trout swimming deep
pools in Gumlog Creek. They cling, they sway in ecstasy
of guilt. A rumble groans beneath the logs, a grinding
of stones stacked three deep beneath a corner. Slowly,
the church leans, slowly west it slides. "A sign, a sign!
Oh God, convict us of our sins! Old Jonah knew, he knew!
Jehovah spit us from the belly of the fish that we may
save our souls, go preach the word in Nineveh! Repent!"
The congregation lies in heaps against the western wall,
afraid to move lest He should bring the mountain down as well.
"Crawl, my brethren, crawl to God!" Enoch leads the way
across the tilting floor until the church rocks back.
"Amiracle, my brethren, let us sing a verse "Just As I Am,"
and pray for fish to swallow us whene're we stray again!"

VI. ISAIAH TREED

"...and all liars, shall have their part
in the lake that burneth with fire
and brimstone." Enoch pounds his text
into the far corners of the church—
the back corner where Ike tugs the collar
of his shirt, feels the lie around his neck
like a burning rope soaked in coal oil.
The stink of brimstone fills his throat;
his cheeks know Enoch's eyes, cold fire
accusing, commanding that he rise, come
forward, and repent. The mourner's bench
looms large, fills the church from front
to back, pushes Ike through the door and,
running, down the path to Gumlog Creek.
There the big oak, full with July, beckons—
and he climbs, up, up until the limbs grow
small, and he can wrap his arms around
the trunk, press his burning face against
the scratchy bark. He hears a rustling
from the creek below, a low chant moaning,
rising, ever rising: "Come, Isaiah, come
to God. Repent your sins. Repent!"
The rough bark moves beneath his skin;
leaves flicker toward his head like flames.

MIRACLE AT RAVEN GAP

"If I could have a mess of greens
just once before I die."
Old Mary Dean lies pale and thin,
her kinfolk standing by.

"I've got a patch of turnips, Min,
don't guess they'll hurt her none.
I'll fry a pone of cornbread too,
be back here when the sun

sets down in Raven Gap." So Nell
went home and fixed a plate
for Mary Dean's last dying wish—
and with a will she ate.

Next morning, Nell thought ghosts could walk.
She started, gave her head a scratch
when out her window saw at dawn
Old Mary digging in her turnip patch.

THE MIDWIFE

No question who had fathered this one.
Mary Nash rocks back on aching knees,
continues tidying up the job she's done
of catching Lena Mathis' son. A long night
this, and more than ample time to hear
the name thrust out between clenched teeth,
a name that Mary knows too well from twenty
years of sleeping in his bed. My Cal, she
thinks, and I have given him no son but this
I claim with no part but my hands, my skill
in birthing other women's sons. She ties
the dark cord, cuts it neat, and binds
the little belly tight. Poor mite, he'll have
no name but Lena Mathis' son, the one who looks
so much like Calvin Nash, they'll say. She lays
him, swaddled now, beside his mother's arm,
and, turning, reaches shaking hands for coffee
simmering in the black pot on the hearth.

NOVEMBER WIND

An early winter cold
hums around Granny Knob,
sets the Cabin hissing
like a woman
barely holding her peace.
Her tongue flicks edges
of a mouth dry, set white
above the lip.
Molly turns her back,
drags the dishrag
hard across a table
clean already.
Water roils in the pan,
splashes beside tears
on the scrubbed-pine floor.
She will not speak;
it is not permitted,
but when she takes her bed,
her back will offer him
silence
echoing the clatter
of polished pans
in a too-clean room.

FOOL'S GOLD

Salathiel John never looks on a stranger
but he tilts his black hat,
potential danger to that man's gold
if he cuts the cards from Salathiel's hand,
engages him in stud or draw.

Salathiel John never left Brasstown Valley
but once, for nearby Auraria—
where wealth, so they said,
was there for the digging up any draw.
He found fool's gold and a deck of cards,
grew a fulsome beard, bought a soft black hat,
learned that cutting the cards was an easier row
than digging for gold, or in Brasstown for corn.

Now he sits by the oak where the trail
from Auraria turns west toward the mountain,
sits fanning his cards in a nonchalant way.
He tips his black hat, speaks to any man passing
in the softest of tones. He keeps his gold
in a brown leather pouch he made from the hide
of a buck he found up a draw in Auraria,
up the draw in Auraria where he learned to play stud.

JACOB'S CAUSE

War done, feet horned from trails long winding down
through Nantahala's Gorge to Double Knob and home,
Jacob rocks as he will rock for thirty years and more.
No plowing now, he's done his share in battles
fought from First Bull Run to White Oak Swamp
with Stonewall Jackson and his mighty troop.
When neighbors pass along the path that winds
below the Knob and down along Corn Creek, he hails:
"Neighbor, come and set a spell. Have I told you
how we whupped them damned blue-bellies good
and captured what we didn't downright kill?
Old Stonewall said we wuz the best he ever saw,
us boys from out these hills with eyes so sharp
as ever dropped a squirrel from pine or oak
or stopped a horse thief in his tracks." Antietam,
Jacob's red-bone hound lies, yawning, by his side.
His paws run rabbits in his sleep while Jacob rocks,
slow, then faster, faster as the battle rages on.
Old Stonewall take Manassas Junction once again.

WARTS FOR PARALEE

"Paralee's a witch, Mae. She'll conjure off
your warts. We'll hide beside the lower road."
Two little girls peer down the rutted track
where mountains turn to valley fields, look west

to see the woman, old and humped, leaning on her cane.
Her eyes are light, strange light that burns Mae's
hands, trembling now but willing to be warmed
by any touch that might take horny lumps away. Eyes

burn through laurel clumps where two girls hide; eyes
swing away. She limps on down the track toward Lee's
where she will knock three times, and ask a bed tonight.

ELLIE'S NEIGHBORS
I. MARY'S APPLES

That rag-tag and bob-tail over at the other side
of the valley can't keep outta grief. That Mary's
done it this time, gone and broke her leg chasing
after one of Sudie's younguns. Serves her right,
old witch, always yelling when they come by
her house. Like she was God of Brasstown.
Don't want nothin' or nobody touching what's hers.
She acts like every stick she owns is the Ark
of the Covenant—and she'll be struck dead one day
for blasphemy, she will. Her apples, indeed! Like
God made Eden just for her, and Sudie's pore younguns
weren't to come near it. Just because she come here
first, she thinks that every spoonful of earth from
Double Knob to Raven Cliffs was made for her benefit!
You'd think that line from the thunderstruck oak
to Corn Creek was drawed by Moses with a golden stick
to keep the rest of us from crossing to the upper gap.
Why, just the other day, I seen her beating Lymon Shockley's
pig because he sniffed her steps and nosed around her tree.
And then chewed Lymon out—for owning a pig! I swear,
I just can't get nothin' done for watching what she does!

II. NAOMI'S NERVE

Naomi Davis died this morning, did ya hear?
Now, there was a woman with nerve! Some past
ninety she was, and it forty year since she fought
the wolves all night. I remember hearing how she
throwed rocks to keep 'em off her calves over
by Lick Log Creek. Ain't been no wolves around
here in many a year, but I heard tell of times
when they run in packs all through these hills—
stole stock and younguns too, if'n they was left
alone too long. Usta be powerful bad over to
Lick Log, drawed by all that Davis stock, I
rightly suspicion. And no man on the place the night
Naomi fought! Them Davis men was bad to wander—
allus flitting off over the Gap for some cause
or nother, they was. Naomi never said a word,
though; all them Davises has some pride to burn,
would of let them wolves tear their throat afore
they'd speak any word to let the family down.
I don't doubt none they'll bury Naomi proud.

III. AN AWFUL SORRY MAN

That Homer's mean, Amanda, mean as sin!
Allus tell, anybody with squinchey little eyes
can't be nothing else. Come into the store
t'other day, seen Lem Sykes buying some sugar,
knocked the poke out'n his hand and taken his
place at the counter. Just as ornery
as an upland rattler in a dry spell, I swear!
His pore mama died when he was no more'n three,
left them four boys to raise theyselves. Run
wild, that passel of younguns did, run wild!
Growed up big and mean—half the folks round
Wolf Pen Gap can testify to that. And that
pore wife of his'n, don't know why she up
and wedded such a sorry man. Many's the day
I seen her with both eyes blackened and she ain't
hardly got no teeth left. Looks like she would
of taken a stick of stovewood and frailed
the daylights outta him! He ain't worth the powder
and shot to kill him, may I drop dead if'n I lie!

IV. CHARLIE LEECH'S WIVES

Sudie, look at that string of younguns coming
into preaching, tripping behind that Charlie
like a covey of quail skittering acrosst
the pasture. I swear, that man's got a finger
in more than one pie! Niece, indeed! She don't
look like no Leech I ever saw, nor none
of his mother's kin neither. When she come
here to help out Lena, and her down with low blood,
I had my suspicions then. Now, for sure, there's
three more younguns since she came, and Lena
allus ailing. I ain't seen her up and about
these four years past, but that Serena's been
to preaching twicet and more with a new brood—
just like her, squinchey eyes and scrawny hair.
I heard too that Charlie killed some sixteen hogs
this winter past, and don't you tell me Lena's
young needs any ways that kinda meat! I wandered
over towards Turkey Buzzard Gap just t'other day,
seen Serena pranching around in the back lot
like she owned the place. Counted six yard younguns
too. I swear, Sudie, that's too many for one woman,
and her been down this long with that low blood!

V. THE BRAGGART

Look at that Abe Carpenter go swaggering by,
I swear, that's the braggingest man I've seed!
Luke heard him running off last week as to how
he'd killed over a hundred bucks in his life,
and none of them with less'n seven points, too.
I bet if 'n he was Samson, he'd of slew twicet
as many of them Philistines as that Samson
done, or more'n twicet, to hear him telling it!
Ain't nobody in this valley gonna believe him
and his tale about how he fought The War. Why,
he couldn't even of been borned when them old
English come and tried to make us some of
their'n. Must of been some yarn his grandaddy
told—though, if 'n that old man fought anything
fiercer'n a rocking chair, I'd eat my bonnet!
All "say-so" and no "do-so" them Carpenters, each
and ever one of them. And Abe the worst, for sure!
Hear him tell it, he's been clean to that Pacific
Ocean and back, killing Indians all the way, scalp'n
them too, though if 'n them ain't coon pelts he's
got
hanging on his wall, I'll salt and pepper my best
Sunday apron, and eat it ever living scrap!

VI. A THREAT OF BLACK EYES

I seen him, Sudie, seen that pore Lee boy
over to Aunt Liddie's! Went and hanged
hisself, he did, on one of them big oaks
out behind her barn. They say he was desperate
over that snippy Jenkins gal over by Lick Log,
been casting sheep's eyes at him these two
years past, she has. I seen her at preaching—
taking in ever thing in pants, them as are free
and them tied as well. Ain't no better'n she
should of been, that gal! Can't be no more'n
sixteen neither, flirting round ever since
she was less'n ten. Them black eyes sneaking
out'n the ruffles on her bonnet like a pair
of chickadees a-courtin' in a budding sycamore.
I swear, ain't no woman's man safe when such
as that is free to run loose in this valley!

34

LIZA'S MONDAY

She has left her tubs and boiling sheets, fled
north across the woodlot, heard no grumble
from the pigs as she passed, the chicken shed
where eggs wait to be gathered, felt

no pain as December's harsh wind dried
lye soap on her arms, reddened hands held
stiff by her sides, palms forward as to catch
the gusts that sweep the slopes of Double Knob.

Inside the cabin: Ethan's shirt to patch,
the fire to mend, small Issac sleeping
in his crib, soon to wake for nursing.
These and other chores are in her keeping,

but she hurries up the mountainside
as on an April day to search for mint
and cress, to find first violets that hide
in white and purple patches by Corn Creek.

The ridge is steep and rocky, sharp with briars.
Raked inside by gales howling bleak
as northern winds around the cabin whine,
she does not feel the laurel tug her dress,

the briars pricking dark red beads that shine
on bare arms. All winter afternoon she climbs
until she gains the highest rocks, the knobs
where one can look out, trace the spines

of distant mountains, scan the valley floor—
black dots for shed and cabin, smoke only wisps
blown by the wind. Lisa sees no more:
not broken stones underfoot, not heavy sky

holding snow. She sits on Double Knob, back
against the ledge, and watches night come by
to close the valley, wipe her clearing out
as though it has never been. Snow clouds

roil around Liza's head, wrap cold arms about
bent shoulders, fill her aproned lap, open hands,
Below, the wash-fire has burned down to embers;
Ethan long begun the search across his lands.

Photograph by Linda Segars

Bettie Sellers, Goolsby Professor of English at Young Harris College, Georgia, has lived and worked for more than twenty years in the hills and valleys where her great-grandfather was a circuit-riding Methodist preacher. Raised on stories of this Appalachian region told by her maternal grandmother, she approaches her subject with experience and understanding. She has won many awards for her previous books: Author of the Year in Poetry, 1979, for SPRING ONIONS AND CORNBREAD, The Dixie Council of Authors of Journalists; Poet of the Year, 1979, The Southeastern Writers Association; Author of the Year in Poetry, 1982, for MORNING OF THE RED-TAILED HAWK, The Dixie Council of Authors and Journalists; The Caroline Wyatt Memorial Award for the unpublished manuscript of LIZA'S MONDAY, 1984, The Atlanta Writers Club, and most recently, The Daniel Whitehead Hicky Memorial National Award for "O Absalom, My Son, My Son" from LIZA'S MONDAY.

Mother of three, grandmother of four, Bettie Sellers teaches English and travels the Southeast giving poetry readings, workshops and lecture in schools and colleges.

APPALACHIAN CONSORTIUM PRESS
Boone, North Carolina

The Appalachian Consortium Press is a division of the Appalachian Consortium Incorporated, specializing in the publication of carefully produced books of particular interest to Southern Appalachia. The Press is controlled by the Publications Committee and the Board of Directors, the members of which are appointed by the Chief Administrative Officers of the member institutions and agencies of the corporation.

Appalachian State University   Lees-McRae College
Blue Ridge Parkway   Mars Hill College
East Tennessee State University   Mountain Regional Library

APPALACHIAN CONSORTIUM

N. C. Division of Archives & History   Warren Wilson College
Southern Highland Handicraft Guild   Western Carolina University
United States Forest Service   Western N. C. Historical Assoc.
Great Smoky Mountains Natural History Association